THE HISTORY OF FOODS
FAST FOOD

by Kristine Spanier, MLIS

pogo

Ideas for Parents and Teachers

Pogo Books let children practice reading informational text while introducing them to nonfiction features such as headings, labels, sidebars, maps, and diagrams, as well as a table of contents, glossary, and index.

Carefully leveled text with a strong photo match offers early fluent readers the support they need to succeed.

Before Reading

- "Walk" through the book and point out the various nonfiction features. Ask the student what purpose each feature serves.
- Look at the glossary together. Read and discuss the words.

During Reading

- Have the child read the book independently.
- Invite them to list questions that arise from reading.

After Reading

- Discuss the child's questions. Talk about how they might find answers to those questions.
- Prompt the child to think more. Ask: Were you surprised to learn the first fast food restaurants are more than 100 years old? What foods do you think should be served faster?

Pogo Books are published by Jump!
3500 American Blvd W, Suite 150
Bloomington, MN 55431
www.jumplibrary.com

Copyright © 2026 Jump!
International copyright reserved in all countries. No part of this book may be reproduced in any form without written permission from the publisher.

Jump! is a division of FlutterBee Education Group.

Library of Congress Cataloging-in-Publication Data

Names: Spanier, Kristine, author.
Title: Fast food / by Kristine Spanier, MLIS.
Description: Minneapolis, MN: Jump!, Inc., [2026]
Series: The history of foods | Includes index.
Audience: Ages 7–10
Identifiers: LCCN 2024054560 (print)
LCCN 2024054561 (ebook)
ISBN 9798892139120 (hardcover)
ISBN 9798892139137 (paperback)
ISBN 9798892139144 (ebook)
Subjects: LCSH: Fast food restaurants—United States—History—Juvenile literature. | Restaurateurs—United States—Biography—Juvenile literature.
Classification: LCC TX945.3 .S73 2026 (print)
LCC TX945.3 (ebook)
DDC 647.9573–dc23/eng/20241205
LC record available at https://lccn.loc.gov/2024054560
LC ebook record available at https://lccn.loc.gov/2024054561

Editor: Jenna Gleisner
Designer: Molly Ballanger

Photo Credits: M. Unal Ozmen/Shutterstock, cover; Keith Homan/Shutterstock, 1; oasisamuel/Shutterstock, 3; Ken Wolter/Shutterstock, 4; Fort Worth Star-Telegram/Tribune News Service/Getty, 5; Security Pacific National Bank Collection/Los Angeles Public Library, 6-7; Everett Collection Historical/Alamy, 8; Nataliia K/Shutterstock, 8 (frame); UPI/Alamy, 9; Retro AdArchives/Alamy, 10-11 (ad); Shutterstock, 10-11 (fries); wk1003mike/Shutterstock, 10-11 (background); Leila Grossman/Getty, 12-13; pjohnson1/iStock, 13; San Francisco Chronicle/Hearst Newspapers/Getty, 14-15; FabrikaCr/iStock, 16 (wrap); Yuliia Davydenko/Dreamstime, 16 (yogurt); LauriPatterson/iStock, 16 (salad); Deutschlandreform/Shutterstock, 17, 18 (sandwich); pancha.me/Shutterstock, 18 (coffee cup); jack-sooksan/Shutterstock, 18-19; yan4ik/Adobe Stock, 20; dlyastokiv/Adobe Stock, 20; Tada Images/Shutterstock, 20-21; Prachana Thong-on/Shutterstock, 23.

Printed in the United States of America at Corporate Graphics in North Mankato, Minnesota.

TABLE OF CONTENTS

CHAPTER 1
Faster Food 4

CHAPTER 2
More Choices 8

CHAPTER 3
Fast Food Chain Changes 16

QUICK FACTS & TOOLS
Timeline 22
Glossary 23
Index 24
To Learn More 24

CHAPTER 1
FASTER FOOD

Have you seen a White Castle? This was the first fast food **chain** in the United States.

It opened in 1921 in Wichita, Kansas. Workers cooked hamburgers fast. They were only five cents each!

CHAPTER 1

The Pig Stand opened in 1921, too. It was in Dallas, Texas. It sold smoked pork sandwiches. It was the first **drive-in**. More people owned cars in the early 1920s. **Carhops** delivered food to cars! People stayed in their cars to eat.

> ### WHAT DO YOU THINK?
>
> Roy Allen sold root beer from a stand. He partnered with Frank Wright. In 1923, they opened A&W. This chain sells food and root beer. The name came from the first letters of their last names. What would you name a restaurant? Why?

CHAPTER 1

CHAPTER 2
MORE CHOICES

Richard and Maurice McDonald were brothers. In 1940, they opened a drive-in. It was in California. They prepared burgers in an **assembly line**. It was simple and fast. **Customers** walked to the window to order. They were served in just 20 seconds!

Ray Kroc saw how successful McDonald's was. He helped the brothers **franchise**. This meant people paid them to open more locations. In 1961, Kroc bought the business. By 1984, there were 7,500 McDonald's worldwide!

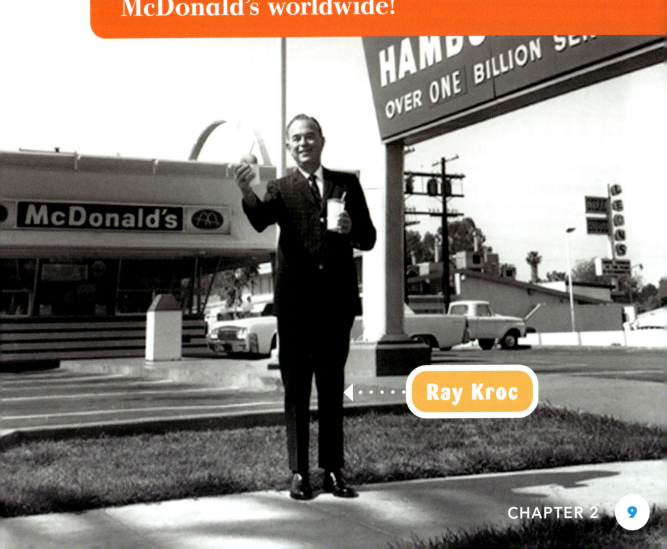

Ray Kroc

CHAPTER 2

Insta-Burger King opened in Florida in 1953. The next year, Dave Edgerton and James McLamore bought it. They shortened the name to Burger King.

In 1957, McLamore **invented** the Whopper. It was much bigger than other burgers at the time.

WHAT DO YOU THINK?

The Whopper is named for its size. What sandwich would you invent? What would you call it? Why?

1970s advertisement

CHAPTER 2

11

Colonel Harland Sanders

Fast food is not just burgers! Colonel Harland Sanders had a restaurant in Corbin, Kentucky. He created a secret **recipe** for fried chicken. It was a blend of 11 herbs and spices. He started a chain called Kentucky Fried Chicken. The first one opened in 1952. Now, this chain is called KFC.

CHAPTER 2

Glen Bell opened the first Taco Bell in 1962 in California. He named it after himself! It was the first fast food chain to sell Mexican food.

> **DID YOU KNOW?**
>
> The first Subway opened in 1965. This chain serves fresh sandwiches. People choose what they want on their sandwiches.

CHAPTER 2

CHAPTER 2

CHAPTER 3
FAST FOOD CHAIN CHANGES

In the early 2000s, fast food chains added healthier options to their menus. Some began selling fresh fruit and salads.

New chains became popular. Panera Bread was one. It sells sandwiches, salads, and soups. Food is made fresh when it is ordered.

CHAPTER 3   17

Coffee shops have entered the fast food race, too! Starbucks opened its first shop in Seattle, Washington, in 1971. By 2003, it had 7,225 stores worldwide. The company began selling breakfast sandwiches that year. These were so popular that lunch items were added. Now, there are more than 36,000 Starbucks around the world!

TAKE A LOOK!

Chains are ranked by sales. What were the top 20 fast food chains in the United States in 2024? Take a look!

1	McDONALD'S	
2	STARBUCKS	
3	CHICK-FIL-A	
4	TACO BELL	
5	WENDY'S	
6	DUNKIN'	
7	BURGER KING	
8	SUBWAY	
9	CHIPOTLE	
10	DOMINO'S	
11	PANERA BREAD	
12	PANDA EXPRESS	
13	PIZZA HUT	
14	SONIC DRIVE-IN	
15	POPEYES LOUISIANA KITCHEN	
16	KFC	
17	DAIRY QUEEN	
18	ARBY'S	
19	JACK IN THE BOX	
20	PAPA JOHNS	

Our world is changing. Fast food chains are, too. Some have ordering **kiosks**. People can also order food from **apps**. Do you have a favorite restaurant? Is it a fast food chain?

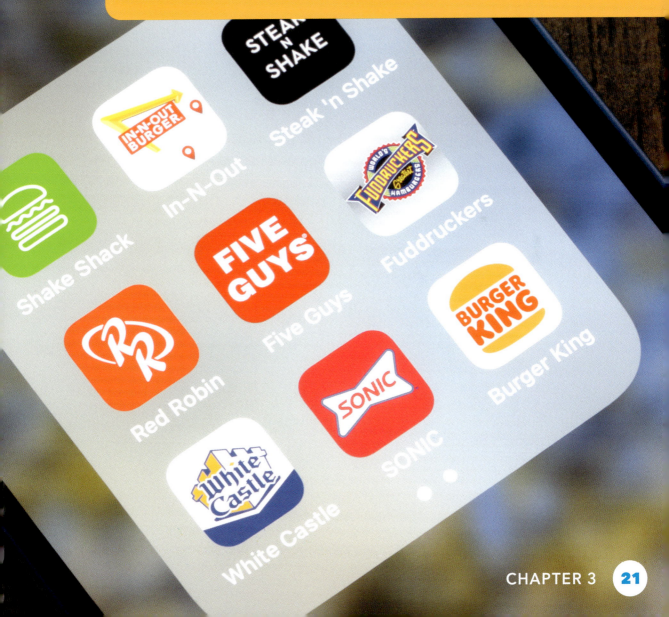

CHAPTER 3 21

QUICK FACTS & TOOLS

TIMELINE

Take a look at some important dates in the history of fast food!

1921
The first White Castle opens in Wichita, Kansas.

1921
The Pig Stand opens in Dallas, Texas. It is the first drive-in.

1923
The first A&W opens in Sacramento, California.

1961
Ray Kroc buys McDonald's.

1940
Richard and Maurice McDonald open the first McDonald's in San Bernardino, California.

1952
Harland Sanders franchises the first Kentucky Fried Chicken in Salt Lake City, Utah.

1953
The first Insta-Burger King opens in Jacksonville, Florida.

1962
Glen Bell opens the first Taco Bell in Downey, California.

1965
The first Subway opens in Bridgeport, Connecticut.

1971
The first Starbucks opens in Seattle, Washington.

2022
More than 265,000 fast food restaurants are open in the United States.

GLOSSARY

apps: Computer programs that perform certain tasks.

assembly line: An arrangement of machines and workers in which a product passes from one person or machine to the next, with each performing a small, separate task, until it is completely assembled.

carhops: People who bring food to customers in their cars at drive-in restaurants.

chain: A group of restaurants owned by the same company that offers the same menu items.

customers: People who buy things from a particular restaurant or business.

drive-in: A restaurant designed so that customers may be served in their cars.

franchise: To sell the right to someone to sell a product or service.

invented: Created and produced for the first time.

kiosks: Small structures often used as stands for selling something.

recipe: Instructions for preparing food, including what ingredients are needed.

INDEX

Allen, Roy 6
A&W 6
Bell, Glen 14
Burger King 10, 20
drive-in 6, 8, 20
Edgerton, Dave 10
fruit 16
hamburgers 5, 8, 10, 13
Kentucky Fried Chicken 13, 20
Kroc, Ray 9
McDonald brothers 8, 9
McDonald's 9, 20

McLamore, James 10
Panera Bread 17, 20
Pig Stand 6
salads 16, 17
Sanders, Harland 13
sandwiches 6, 10, 14, 17, 18
Starbucks 18, 20
Subway 14, 20
Taco Bell 14, 20
White Castle 4, 5
Whopper 10
Wright, Frank 6

TO LEARN MORE

Finding more information is as easy as 1, 2, 3.

❶ Go to www.factsurfer.com
❷ Enter "fastfood" into the search box.
❸ Choose your book to see a list of websites.